GET OUT & STAY OUT

DAVID KIRK

DEDICATION

This book is dedicated to the convict that wants to drop that title and be just a man among men.

CONTENTS

ACKNOWLEDGMENTS

I want to acknowledge all of the men I have discussed this topic with who have told me their stories. I also want acknowledge my mother who was on my side even when I wasn't.

Every person who has helped me along the way, there are way too many to list… Thank you.

1 WHO AM I AND WHERE AM I FROM

My name is David Kirk and I grew up in southern California in the late 70's and 80's. this was a time of partying and utter disregard for the rules at school and laws of my state.

As a boy I started to disassociate with my family because my priority was partying and having fun. My parents tried to address these incidents as they came up and would put me on restriction or use the paddle or the brush to try and impose their will.

I was never then and am still not now ok with anyone putting their hands on me in that way.

Now am I saying it was inappropriate, well yes, but it was not for no reason. I had very little respect for others and others possessions and was an extremely intelligent kid. That combination is a recipe for conflict in the home.

I was caught with my first bag of weed, by a cop, when I was in 4th or 5th grade. I got it from someone older who told me "if you get caught with this you can't tell anyone where you got it". I got caught and held my mud because I was built that way, us against them.

Partying and a real disregard for societal rules and customs left me free to decide how life was to be with no parental input. There was no one telling me to moderate. My friends were kids too and we just made it up as we went.

By the time I was 14 I knew I would be going to prison. I never considered changing my path in those days. It aint a crime if you don't get caught was my motto.

Let's fast forward to my 20's. I turned 21 in prison. I remember sitting on my rack listening to my Walkman, Bad

Company – 10 from 6 as the new year passed. I thought I had it going on because I smoked a joint to my head on my rack by myself. The only joint I ever smoked by myself in prison. I felt like I was ballin'.

I was there for a minute when the desire to be different hit. I was walking the yard at CMC west when I realized I no longer wanted to belong with these people. We were looking for a wall to take a photo in front of so we could look hard. We had to take it in front of the racquetball court because the rest of the place is all flowers and rolling hills. It was right around that time I figured I'd just get out and be "normal".

I ran into a pretty big obstacle when I got out. I wanted to make up for lost time. Not with my family but with my friends and partying. Having fun was still the goal I just wanted to not go back to prison so I decided to get a job because that's what "normal" people do.

I got & lost a string of jobs because I could not be a good employee. I had never learned about that. I'm sure someone tried to teach it, I just wasn't having any of that work bullshit. It got in the way of my partying.

Long story short, I absconded and moved out of state. In my mind I let myself off parole and started over in a new place. You can probably guess the parole board had other plans for H05305, that was my number.
When I got picked up in Alabama for being out of bounds they flew me home (shacked and leg irons on three different planes) and gave me 6 months and then let me go.

This is when I began trying to learn how to stay out.

There are some basic things that people learn as they grow up and learn from their parents and teachers. These lessons are all stackable.

What I mean by stackable is you have to learn lesson number 1 before you can move on to lesson 2 and you must know lesson 1 & 2 before you can learn lesson 3.

Looking back that is such a simple concept. For a person with a huge ego that is a real challenge. I had never accomplished anything that I could be really proud of yet I had an ego the size of Texas.

This was the one thing that would consistently get in my way – my ego & pride. If you are honest with yourself you may find this is true for you.

There were times that very successful people took an interest in helping me. I would listen to what they had to say and be polite but as soon as they walked away I would think "what does that guy know".

I still thought very highly of myself and thought I was smarter than most everyone else..

Even when my ignorance of how life worked was glaring me in the face.

While not being able to support myself without committing crime I would think that someone who was responsible and self-supporting was somehow dumber than I was or didn't get it.

This takes a special kind of ego. More in the self-delusion category probably.

So to recap who am I and where I'm from:
I was a low level criminal with the ego of a self-made millionaire… except I would become periodically homeless. Not sleep outside mind you – just mooch off my friends for a place to stay so it never registered that I was homeless. I lied to myself all the time by blaming others for my circumstances.

That is a perfect example of not _truly_ looking at the situation I was in.
Self-dilution is the first mode of operation we must discard to succeed. There are others but this is #1. An honest look at what you are working with as a person. You may not like everything you see but you need to see it to fix it.

I will be discussing that at great length in the book. This is the first building block of the foundation you will be building your new freedom filled life upon. Don't gloss over it when it comes, without sorting this part out you will be destined to fail yet again. It aint a maybe.

So if you are ready to become a productive member of society then you are saying you are capable of taking an honest look at yourself and locate the issues that are getting in the way of your success. _The real issues._

You are saying that what you have been doing is no longer producing acceptable results and you are willing to think differently. To learn a new way by gathering information and making yourself act differently. To do the work required to act and more importantly think differently.

If it sounds like you won't be you anymore don't worry, you will still be you. You will still have the same sense of humor, like all the same foods and have the same hobbies. You will just be removing the things that have gotten in the way of your success in life. One or two things at a time.

This life changing shift in my thinking was a process, it didn't happen overnight. I made a bunch of mistakes along the way.

I will tell you that I no longer hold my shoulders up when I walk or have a gangster lean. I no longer wear dickies and a white t-shirt every day as if was my uniform.
The fellas I did my time with would not recognize the man I am today.
I'm now that straight guy with a job and family, that I support. Kids that I parent and a job that is a career.

"Hey wood, how about kicking us a few smokes so the fellas can smoke after chow"

I am no longer a torpedo.

Keep in mind I'm not an educated man. My writing is way below the level of professional. I'm sure my punctuation is jacked and only the words that had a red line under them get corrected if spelled wrong…

It's the information in this book that can help open you mind like mine was opened. That is the important stuff.

2 IT STARTS BEFORE R&R

So there are a few things that I want to point out that I have seen become obstacles to myself and the hundreds of men I have observed attempt to make this change.

1) Most convicts trust themselves more than anyone else in the world. (even though they lie to themselves)
2) Most men getting out of prison have no new information to go on, they are going to just "do better" this time.
3) Most convicts try for the most freedom right from the gate
4) Most convicts prioritize everything for short term payoff.
5) Most convicts are overconfident in their own ability to follow an action plan

You know it is funny, you could substitute teenager for convict and we could be having the same discussion.

This is really the crux of the situation. Most convicts have not learned the lessons that are taught to young adults and are stuck in the cycle of try to do better again with the same info and expect it to be different.
Example:
I keep getting fired from my jobs
Convict solution:
Get another job – this is not a complete solution
Real solution:
Figure out what I keep doing to get myself fired – figure out why I keep doing that same thing - usually a belief

system or a work ethic issue. Get to work on changing the way I view the situation.

Get a new job – armed with the new information and action plan.

That is basically how this whole get down works – upgrade the information or action plan and try again.

If it works then move onto the next area in your life that needs new information or a new action plan. If someone got you this book, dude your shit is fucked up…

So let's discuss new information gathering for a minute.

If I do not go outside of myself and get new information I am going to make the same determinations or take the same actions because I'm following what I think is the good plan based on the current information. Just like the last time so there will be no new result.

Think about it for a minute. How many times have we tried the same thing over and over expecting better results? Over and over we have tried to "be good" or "make good choices" but if we are the same person with the same info deciding to try the same action expecting the result to be different this time. We are just wasting our time and effort.

Here are a few pearls I've been told over and over throughout my life.

- Don't like what you are getting, quit doing what you're doing.
- If nothing changes, nothing changes.

- The only way people know your different is when they see you acting different, not when you tell them your different or "IT" will be different.

Ok so now that we know we need new information where do we locate it?

This is where the typical convict has to begin to go against their own instinct of trusting themselves over others, even though they have not been successful.

We need to begin gathering information from people who have what we want. I pick the person based on the topic. If you want to have a great relationship with your wife seek out a man that has what you consider a great relationship with his wife and ask him about relationships. Think about the challenges that you have in this area and discuss those things. For me this has been a man named Mike K.

Now Mike has a great relationship with his wife. The trick is, as far as I can tell, is to give his wife what she needs without her having to ask him for it. This is what makes a relationship work extremely well. Not easy to do. I hear it gets easier as you go along…. I'm still working on that one. The real problem is that I'm not a mind reader so for me to give my girlfriend what she needs without asking me for it means I need to pay attention to her so I can figure that stuff out.

I never used to really pay attention until she was upset. Once she is upset it's too late to avoid the thing. I end up spending time after she is upset and that doesn't help for the next time.

So it turns out I will be spending time on a subject either way so if I change WHEN I spend the time to before she is upset I can avoid it all together.

That is the new information I use to have a better relationship.

It seems very simple and it really is. It is just not that easy. This is how it works on all topics.

Mike has a relationship with his wife that I want mine to be like so I go to him to discuss my relationship and follow his advice. (action plan)

Mike also had tax issues at the time (owed a shit ton of money to the IRS) I was going to him for relationship advice. I didn't go to him for tax advice.

So you see if you find someone who has the info you need on a subject they don't need to be on point on all subjects, just the one you are getting the info on.

Now I'm going to drill down on this a little bit.

Don't get home buying advice from someone who has never bought a home. Seems simple enough right?

So typically we would go to someone whom we know who has bought a house for that advice. That seems pretty self-explanatory.

Keep in mind that buying house is the largest purchase that a person typically makes. Most people I know that own houses have only bought one or two houses in their lifetime.

I would say that marginally gives them experience.

I would say it would be better to go to someone who sells houses for a living and learn from them. They know all of the pitfalls to buying a house and have them memorized. They have sold hundreds of houses and have real experience. Not one or two anxiety filled experiences, hundreds of sales to gather their information. Now that person would be the best home buyer out of the three options I've listed.

I could learn from someone like that things that my sister, who has bought one house, could not know.

That does not mean I don't discuss it with her. It means she has one experience to go off of and can explain how it went for her.

So to recap:

When trying to change a situation you need new updated information (and thought process) to be able to make better choices.

When determining where to get the information look to the "best source" available. **Not just any other information, qualify the source.**

Are they successful in that area of life?

Crete you action plan based on the new information.

(I will be getting into what an action plan is a little later)

Here is where you make a list of people you want to learn topics from. Think about this like it matters, because it does.

Work / Career advice =

_____

Relationship advice =

_____

Parenting advice =

_____

Parole advice =
(agent?)_____

Financial advice =

_____

General life advice =

_____

Life Coach =

_____

——

The life coach position in your life can be anyone who has a good solid all around life. Everyone needs someone, who is successful at life, to keep an eye on their life as they begin to build the new amazing life. In 12 step programs people use a sponsor to monitor there progress and help make adjustments to the game plan. It is the same thing but for the whole life.

I look at a life coach as someone who is a general manager – like on a baseball team. Let's break that down because it works in so many different situations that it obviously is the way to go for a personal life.

I will use a baseball organization as an example:
On the baseball team there are several positions that need to function for the team to be successful.
Starting with the general manager. That person identifies the issues getting in the way of the team's success and has the organization work on those issues. By either upgrading the players skill set or getting rid of players or systems that are no longer producing positive results.

So the general manger is the life coach.
The life coach says you need to become better at hitting, so what now?
We can go to the best hitter on the team and ask him what to do but that's not where the good hitter got their information is it? That guy has been coached and taught how to be a good hitter. Your best bet is to go to where he was taught. Those people are good at teaching hitting. They have a proven track record.

So the life coach says "your weakness in your game is hitting"
This could be any topic in your life.
You go to the coaching staff to learn how to work on the actions you can take to improve your outcome. (he says go to the batting coach and put together and follow an action plan laid out by the coach.
Now you have that information and an action plan to improve.

This is where you and only you have the power to improve. You must follow the action plan to get positive results.

This is the beauty of the situation, your success depends completely on your effort! No one but you can stop you from success.

Now we substitute hitting for keeping a job or anger issues or drugs or whatever is getting in your way.

So I'll lay it out another way.
You meet with your life coach and you both decide you need to work on something. You go fix that issue (with

your "batting" coach) and come back to the life coach and look for what's next.

Eventually there is nothing major left to work on and it becomes fine tuning.

At this point you are having a winning season!!!! An amazing life!!

Let's talk about "action plans".

An action plan is a planned set of actions that you will take on your own.

Action plans will test if what you say you want is what you are willing to work for.

Those are two different things. Everyone wants to be a home run hitter but only people who practice are any good at hitting.

So let's break down an action plan for becoming a better hitter.

We meet with the coaching staff and they determine two issues.

1) I position my feet in the wrong place
2) My bat speed is too slow

The first issue is a simple one to correct. Learn the new position for my feet and make that the new habit. Simple and a small amount of personal effort is required. Take the info and use it (action plan) and eventually, if it is a good action plan, my hitting will improve.

The second issue will take more effort on my part.

I will need to consult a "bat Speed" coach and determine the action plan.

Let's say it includes two things.

1) I will have to train specific muscles to improve my strength so my body can swing faster.
2) I will need to lose 15 lbs. to improve fluidity in my swing

So I go to the weight training staff and get the action plan to improve my strength. I train using the action plan given by the strength coach.

I go to the nutritionist and put together a new weight loss plan that provides the nutrition needed to gain the strength and lose the weight in a healthy way.

The truth is that the hard part is following the action plan. That is the part where you are on your own not eating the cookies because they are not on the list of foods given by the nutritionist. It is in the discipline to follow the action plan, that is where we will find our success. The discipline to make yourself show up to work, no matter what, will change everything in your life if that was an issue.

Once I have begun to see improvements in these two areas there will be a measurable amount of success in my hitting.

That is a blueprint for how to improve everything in your life. It is being used every day in every successful business and personal lives all around the world.

Let's look at an action plan that I have laid out for a guy who typically gets fired for being late or missing work.

Get up an hour earlier than normal.
Get to work 30 minutes early every day.
Show up on all days scheduled.

Now this seems simple and it really is. It took over a year for the guy to be able to consistently do this. He lost 3 jobs in that first year, an improvement from the year before where he had 8 jobs. Now that he has that mastered he has kept his job for 13 years.

So you see the action plan can be very simple but for whatever reason not so easy to follow.

One of the reasons action plans are not followed or do not work is because they are too ambitious. This is because people in general want to jump to the finish line before training for the race.
A good example is parenting. Parents who go to prison have become by default a non-contributing parent at best and another person is raising their kids. Harsh but true.

Every convict I've ever met loves his/her kids. They would kill or die for them no doubt. The problem with that statement is that kids rarely need parents to kill or die for them. What they need is to be loved and to have consistency in their lives.

I hear this all the time "I'm going to be the best dad ever". I think that is a wonderful goal. I think that is what we all strive for.

When your starting line is the "non-existent or in prison parent" you may want to shoot a little lower than "best dad ever". A little more realistic goal is to be a more present parent. I'd say shoot for a decent parent. Once you hit that goal reset you sights on best dad ever!! Progression is key here.

Most people look at situations from their own point of view.

"I've been gone for 5 years and I'm going to……"

May be better to think of you child's experience of you and not tell them what you are going to do to make it up to them. Actions are all that matter.

If you look at their point of view of who you are you may not like what you see.

Kids need positive role models who will spend time with them and answer their questions and play games with them. To be there for them, with solid advice when life gets challenging for them.

If this is not what you have been giving them then you have not been a good parent. It's not a judgement, it's a fact.

So if you have been a non-existent parent I'd say start with being present and a mediocre parent.

Sounds shitty but that's real.

Start there and get to know the person you want to parent because

they have changed since you have been gone.

Consistency is huge to children.

Being able to trust what you say is huge.

Start slow and then ramp up your involvement. Its best for them. Be sure that you can handle the commitment to show up on a regular basis.

The tendency is to start huge then dwindle the effort down to a workable amount of effort. This shows by your actions that you are not reliable. So they learn again you can't be trusted to be there for them.

Don't miss them and promise the world and break their
heart.
Don't feel guilty for leaving and promise the world and
break their heart.

Better to make it every other weekend for 10 years than to
see them inconsistently then disappear again.

So to recap:
Set reasonable goals for yourself.
Don't confuse the desire to be the best dad ever with the
ability to be the best dad ever. You kids will suffer for that
mistake.

3 ALLWAYS BE REAL WITH YOURSELF

This is the part where personal growth can be messy and painful. It's in the messy and painful parts we fix that produce 100% of the growth.
No pain no gain

I'll say that in a different way.

You have to learn to cut through the bullshit that you tell yourself so you can look yourself in the eye, get to the heart of your demons and get them the fuck out of the way.

And yet another way would be ;

Take inventory of who we are and decide what to keep and what to change. I like to think of it in this way. It's a little cold and impersonal but for me that works, no judgement just facts.

Here is the deal, I look at myself like I'm a business. I take an inventory on who I am. My personal traits, strengths and weaknesses. That is who I am in a nut shell. I am a sum of those parts.
I used to be a criminal. I committed crime because I had immediate needs and no way of supporting myself. I was young and on the streets and I liked it.
During that time I came up on some personal skills and traits. Some people call them survival skills. I used those skills to get what I wanted and needed in a partying and criminal environment. I was a kid 15-25 years old.

Well let's take some of those skills and list them so we see what I was working with and how I could apply them in a new way to achieve a positive result.

- I can read the feeling in a room

This comes in handy in prison, drug deal or a business meeting with clients.

- I can tell who the decision makers are in any circumstance

This comes in handy because I am in sales and it helps my closing %

- I understand the law of supply and demand

A joint in the joint is $10.00 and on the street $2.00
So I understand ½ of all business.

- I understand the profit off a bag of weed sold for more than it cost

So I understand the other ½ of all business

- I have had to be manipulative to be given money for drugs

I am quite good at seeing angles that are "out of the box" solutions for business issues as well as seeing strategic liabilities in negotiations and contracts.

So as you can clearly see I have some complex skills that I used as my "survival skills" when a young hoodlum boy that are transferable into my successful life today.

Every single gangster that has been jumped into a gang has been to the toughest business meeting they will ever go to!!!

Discussing a building or a project is easy when everyone is

sure no one gets punched in the face. Talk about high pressure sales meetings. Shit, ever met with a shot caller on a yard before a race riot? If so then you too have been in a business setting where a hostile takeover is eminent.
See where I'm going with this?

So taking an honest look at the skills we have is important. We have to take the good with the bad to start but the first order of business is to determine what the bad is. Here is a list of what I had that was bad inventory that had no redeeming qualities.

- Anger issues
- No work ethic
- Thief – opportunist
- Liar
- Racist

None of those character defects served me in a positive way, ever. Those were all liabilities that got in the way of my success and happiness.
   Without determining the things that are in the way of your happiness you cannot address them. That is just a simple truth. Once you do you begin to build momentum.

   This is how that works, it builds on itself.
   By addressing my anger issues I was better at communicating what I want and need and understanding other people's expectations of me.

That is the payoff to all my effort addressing my anger issues.

Can you imagine how much impact this had in my life? I no longer yell. There is no yelling in my life unless it is at a sporting event. This may seem small, no yelling, and it is. You couple that with all the other little things that you resolve and you remove these liabilities and it's a snowball effect.

Because I communicate better I have a better job. Because I have a better job I have more money. Because I have more money I can relax a little and enjoy things. Because I can relax and enjoy things I am happier. Because I'm happier I am able to sleep better. Because I sleep better I produce more at work making me more money and the snowball starts rolling.

This is what you should take away from this:

- Take an HONEST look at what you are working with.
- Make a list of skills or traits that are positive
- Make a list of the bad – I mean all of it
- Start to act differently when those tendencies come up
- Ride the snowball effect!!!

I know it sounds simple and it truly is as long as we don't get in our own way.

Action plan:

- Do a Google search of "character defects" and print it out.
- Go through them and highlight the ones you have.
- Write down the opposite of the defect next to it.
- Keep this handy and look at it at least 5 times each day

Knowledge really is power if applied.

Here is a list in case you are in prison and cant google anything.

Selfish / Unselfish or Giving or Sharing

Dishonest / Honest

Resentful / Forgiving

Afraid / Faith

Arrogant / Humble

Egotistical / Modest

Cocky / Humble

Envy / Grateful

Sloth / Hard Working/Industrious

Gluttony / Sharing

Impatient / Patient

Vengeful / Loving

Hurtful / Kind

Sarcastic / Complimentary

Intolerant / Tolerant

Hateful / Forgiving or compassionate

Inconsiderate / Considerate

False Pride / Modest

Greedy / Giving

Thieving / Honest & Giving

Lustful / Content

Angry / Happy

Jealous / Secure/Trusting

Procrastination Timely

Self-Seeking/ Charity & Helpful for others

Self-Centered / Selfless & Thoughtful

Self – Righteous / Gracious

Self – Pity Lenient/Positive

Self – Justification / Accepting

Self – Important / Considerate of others

Self – Condemnation / criticism Self – Embracing/ approval

Self – Harming / Self Love

Low Self Esteem / Self-Acceptance

Suspicious / Trusting

Insecure / Secure & Fulfilled

Manipulative / Accepting & truth

Abusive / Caring

Conceited / Unassuming

Non- Committal /Committal

Rationalization / Acceptance of Reality

Judgmental / Fair Minded & Understanding

Denial / Agreeable & Honest

Opinionated / Fair Minded

Violent / Loving

Prejudice / Open Minded

Controlling / Humble

Paranoid / Trusting

Needy / Giving

People Pleasing or Fake / Real & True Self

Unkind / Kind

Irresponsible / Responsible

Perfectionist / Easy Going

Martyr or Victim / Responsible

Infidelity / Monogamous

Enabling / Tough Love

Immoral / Moral or Spiritual

Pompous / Modest

4 RELATIONSHIPS

There are all kinds of relationships. I will focus on two categories.

The first set is personal relationships. These are the relationships that are the most important to human beings. Without them life can become a real struggle to find meaning and drive.

I want to focus on the other persons experience of us, not who we think we are giving them. This is the part where we honestly look at who we have been to these people. Remember that we are not trying to "look" like we are good at this stuff, we are learning to become good at this stuff.

During this process we WANT to find the issues we need to work on.
Making a list of the negative traits is extremely helpful.

I know that some of you are good at some of these already. Only you can run these relationships through the character defect list to see how you really stack up. Remember that the more you find you have to work on the more knowledge you have about yourself. Knowledge + Action = Change.

Also let me say that just because I know about this and have been working on it for years does not mean I'm perfect at it. I still get frustrated with my girlfriend and kids and job and dog... I am reacting better to those situations 90% of the time when they do come up.
The goal is slow steady improvement. So if you are reacting

well to that type of situation 50% of the time that is your starting point. Not good or bad – it just is where you are. We deal in truth.

Now that we have seen how we do on this from our point of view let's examine what the people in our life gets from us.

Personal relationships:
Spouse
Kids
Step kids
In laws
Friends

We need to think about those peoples experience of us. Not who we want them to think we are but who we are to them.

My family had to deal with me disappearing for years. That was their experience of me. When I was around I was hustling or sleeping.

I have spent a lot of time working on my relationships with women.
There are people who are professionals who can help with the other people on the list and to be honest I only have some overview general knowledge. I am not a counselor. I have a therapist and periodically I go when an issue comes up that I need an outside point of view so I don't stay at an impasse.

Each relationship is different and while I know a lot about significant other relationships I am not trying to sound like

I'm a counselor because I'm not.

When they go down the checklist of assets you bring to the table does it include the list of what the spouse values? People place different value on different traits. Women and men are very different.
We need very different things.

This is a huge reason for conflict in a relationship!!!!!
Men try to give their wife what men need because they don't think about what their wife needs. Its instinctive to give the wrong thing. We have to make a conscious effort to give the other person what THEY need and not what WE need.

Example:
Husband and wife disagree on something – men rarely like to discuss things so we avoid the conversation because we assume the wife wants to avoid the conversation. **He gives her what he needs.**
The reality is that she as a women needs to talk about it so **she is not getting what she needs.**
This can snowball when she, as a woman who wants to discuss it, assumes the man wants or needs to discuss it. She tries to discuss it because she needs to but **by doing so gives him what she needs , and not what he needs** which is space. Now there is frustration because the man is trying to avoid the conversation and he is unsuccessful and she keeps trying to discuss it and this frustrated the man.

So we have an issue that needs resolution and two frustrated people. Not a lot of resolution in that situation.

So to say that another way- don't give your spouse what

you need – give them what they need.

No matter how hard you try if you are not giving her / him what they need your effort will make the situation worse.

The key to a happy and compassionate relationship is this.

Men – give your women what they need – not what you need – without making them fight for it.

Women – give your man what he needs – not what you need – without making them fight for it.

I learned this from a relationship seminar a long time ago and it has changed my relationships dramatically.

Review the list of traits that men and women value and see what you do or don't bring to the table.

Top 20 Most Valued Personality Attributes in a Potential Marriage Partner	
What Men Value	**What Women Value**
1) Reliable	1) Warm
2) Warm	2) Reliable
3) Fair	3) Fair
4) Intelligent	4) Intelligent
5) Knowledgeable	5) Knowledgeable
6) Conscientious	6) Trusting
7) Trusting	7) Secure
8) Hardworking	8) Hardworking
9) Secure	9) Emotionally Stable
10) At Ease	10) At Ease
11) Emotionally Stable	11) Perceptive
12) Perceptive	12) Lenient
13) Even-Tempered	13) Conscientious
14) Energetic	14) Energetic
15) Practical	15) Generous
16) Curious	16) Sociable
17) Sociable	17) Curious
18) Creative	18) Well-organized
19) Well-organized	19) Flexible
20) Relaxed	20) Relaxed

Now this is just a generic list off the internet and may or may not have things listed in the order that works for you or your spouse.

Here is an exercise you can try. Both you and your significant other write down the 10 traits that you value. Write them down separately and trade them when you are both done. You may be surprised at how different you value different things.

What I know for sure is that without knowing what our

spouse values most we will think it is what WE value most.

We tend to think everyone thinks like we do, and they don't!!
It took me a long time to figure that out but what a huge difference it made in my life!!

5 BUSINESS RELATIONSHIPS

This is an extremely important lesson if you want to succeed in business.

There are a small minority of people who naturally stand still and keep their mouth shut when they feel uncomfortable. For those people this will be much easier than for the rest of us.

Let's take a look at the things that I see that create an atmosphere of success or failure.

The number one thing I see people do that I believe sets a negative tone when thinking about or speaking about their job is **belittling the position**. What I mean by that is the thought process of "I'm just a _____".
This mentality creates a consistent negative condonation about the position and in turn the persons place in life.

STOP DOING THAT RIGHT NOW!!!
Jobs do not say ANYTHING about our value as human beings.

Lets get that straight right now. There are a lot of people who believe that having a certain position makes you important as a human. Nope, it doesn't work that way.

There are also people who think that the quantity of dollars you have equal your value as a human. Nope, it doesn't work that way either.

If you give of yourself to another there is no higher purpose.

Giving of yourself has no money or college degree or monetary value attached to it.

How you are in the world determines your value as a human.

So armed with that information there is no one above us or below us as people. This is very important to internalize, to know at your core.

The topic for this chapter is business relationships.

It is different in a work setting because we all have different positions within a company.

My boss is above me in my company, he owns the company I work for.

Now to be clear that does not give him more value as a human being in any way. It does mean the position I have in the company is below his position in value. A person in his position created the position I have and gets to say what someone in my position does on a daily basis. They can also ask me to do specific tasks and saying no is insubordination.

So really asking is more like a polite way of telling or a subtle command.

So clearly business is a different eco-system than what I call "real life"

That being said typically it is a good thing to keep relationships at work professional in nature. I am speaking about at first, for the first few years of working with people.

Probably best not to tell that funny story that starts with "This one time in Folsom" or "back when I was tweaking". Most of the people we work with don't have those stories and it is so far out of where they came from it can skew

how they view you before they get to know you.
My boss now knows I've been to prison and had a
substance abuse issue.
I've worked there for 15 years so eventually some things
have come out, long after I was a trusted and proven good
employee.
I do not go into detail. He doesn't need to know any
details, he is my boss.

So let's talk about personal information and coworkers.

Talking to coworkers about personal matters is an
interesting proposition.
Topics need to be rated G. PG after you have been there
for awhile and you get to know people is probably fine.
Rated R topics are definitely to be kept for friends.

When discussing your personal life treat it like a highlight
reel. They don't ever show the dropped balls only the
catches.

This is the appropriate personal information for the
workplace.
My kid plays baseball. We ride dirt bikes. We like to go to
the river. My kid moved up in dirt bike size. We made
homemade pizza and the kitchen was a wreck and it cost
twice as much as buying one… Keep it to topics that you
can't be judged negatively.

Save the drama and bullshit for your friends.
Things to keep to yourself in the work environment.

My brother stole my truck. My parole agent tossed my
house. My ex wife is a *****. I got a homeboy who can get

some dank weed for cheap. I drank way too much last weekend and lost my car.
That crap is for your friends. And if that is your life, you have work to do.

At work people have to listen and have to be polite, they are at work and because of that they are a captive audience. Don't take that as an invitation to ear hump them about your baby mama or your new girlfriend or how your parole agent is being an asshole...

The less negative or drama you bring to work the less negative people attach to what they think about you.

Remember you are not there to make friends. You are there to make money and to learn the next lesson you need to learn so protect your position by keeping how people view you as a positive.

A few key points to remember about your job.

You applied for the job be grateful that they have work for you.
If you don't like how much money you are making get a new job that pays more.
If you want to make friends don't do it at work, join a club or something.
Never sleep with a coworker! I don't care what the situation is. If it goes sideways it will be a thing.

6 CONNECTING WITH SOCIETY

I have worked with many men who have gotten out of prison or gotten sober. In the years that I have been doing this work there is a specific change that I've see happen in the men who become what I call successful.

There is an acceptance that there is no one to blame but themselves for the life they live.

There is a power that comes when being the victim is discarded.
Also there is a change in structure when we are up front about whose fault our life is. Lets be very clear, good or bad, it is your fault.

I go to a 12 step program, due to the traditions of that program I cannot sat which one. There is a step in all of the 12 step programs that explains how I have a part in every single thing that has happened in my life. That step is step #4. In the big book of alcoholics anonymous, which all 12 step programs are based on, it is spelled out in columns. I recommend picking up that book and finding the formula they have for finding your part. It literally is the key to success and happiness.

You don't have to be an alcoholic for the 12 steps to work in your life. The only reference to alcohol is in the first step. You can swap the word alcohol for any other thing you want to work on and the rest of the steps will get you there.

There is a freedom that I received by finding my part in everything that happens, good or bad, in my life.

The victim says if only they didn't fire me, I'd have a job.
I say if I would have followed what I was supposed to do completely they would not have fired me.

Here is an example that I've seen time and time again.
At my work technicians need to be working at 7:00am.
We have had many guys for whom this is a major challenge. They are 5 minutes late on a consistent basis or will be at the shop but still need to change out of tennis shoes and into work boots at 7:00am.

Here is what they guys think:
Its only 5 minutes what's the big deal.

Here is the reality:
They don't care enough about their job to be there working at 7:00am.

Another thing that happens is guys are there dressed and ready to go and they stand around bullshitting. Well, that is stealing money from the company. If you want to bullshit with coworkers for half an hour be at work at 6:30am and there is no issue.

We fire people over that shit. We talk to them once or maybe twice but this isn't friendship, its business. Stealing from your company in any capacity is grounds for termination.

I hear it because I have to drive them home sometimes, dude I was 5 minutes late… bullshit you were 5 minutes late 10 times in two months. Clearly its not important to be there on time. We will find someone who can perform the position as laid out in the job description.

Here is the thing about business, It's not personal. You hear that in movies when the coke dealer smokes his friend for getting high on the dealers coke.
What does it really mean? There is a job description and you had the position and you failed to keep up you end of the bargain.

There is actually a term for this. It's called bringing someone to choice.
There are whole books written on this and this is the basic premise is the viewpoint of any situation;

If you are constantly late to work and you get fired did you really get fired or did you quit by being late all the time? I say you quit by not performing the duties of the position you were hired for.

Here is where all the freedom to succeed comes from!!!
If its your fault, you can choose to better next time!

Lets stick with that scenario, being late. It is the employees responsibility to be there working at 7:00am. That all no other alternative is acceptable to have this position.

There are a million things that can make someone late.
The company does not give a shit about why if it is a consistent thing it's your fault.

They are all excuses.

Sleep through my alarm – don't care - get a better system to wake up

Kids are slow getting ready – not my problem- get them up an hour earlier

Traffic is heavy and unpredictable- don't care – leave earlier

Busses are late – don't give a shit – take the earlier one

Couldn't find my keys – seriously – get 10 sets made just incase

Blah blah blah. Excuse, excuse, excuse.

In business systems are important. If it is a one off thing being late it not an issue.

I have been late to work and its no big deal. I have been late to work less than 10 times in 15 years.

I have been early every day, except for the few days I have been late, for 15 years. If I'm late it's not a thing because it rarely happens. No one mentions it. It doesn't stress me out. It literally doesn't matter. I have a reputation for being early so it's a non-issue.

It's my fault that no one cares if I'm late. I made it so by showing up about an hour early just about every day for years.

Notice this point, I set that up by being early for a long time before I was ever late. I built credit basically by being early.

Believe me when I say I was not always this type of employee.

For many years I was the guy who woke up thinking "how am I going to get out of work today".

I would lie to my work and call in sick.

If I had done that so much to be afraid I'd get fired for calling in I'd go in and pretend to be sick and then go home. Trying to create the illusion that I was a good employee but I really was sick.

I have pretended to be injured to be able to go home.

I have actually injured myself so that I could get a few days off.

I have abandoned more jobs than I care to count because I just could not make myself go.

It was by taking a real honest look at the fact that my life was my fault that I was able to make some real and permanent changes to my life.

Sometimes quickly and sometimes slowly but if we work at this we will begin to make big deal changes.

Here are some things I learned by being truly honest with myself.

I cannot be on drugs and be successful in anything.

I cannot lie and have self-respect.

I don't know everything I thought I knew.

I need people and new information to help me learn.

My survival skills have kept me in mental prison.

I'm extremely intelligent and can be very wrong about something.

I'm very emotional and feel my feeling very strongly.

Not everyone thinks like I do.

Not everyone values the same things I do.

Life is slow and success is built not "got".

Someone else's success does not diminish my own achievements.

I have value as a human being.

Facing these things was much easier than I thought it would be.
I'd known I'd been a fuck up for years and years before I started trying to change. It was no surprise that my thinking and view of the world was a little sideways.

Once I accepted that this train wreck of a life I was living was all my fault and I decided to do something about it help just showed up.

When I truly wanted to change how I was AND was willing to trust the process things began happening that had never happened before.
People out of the blue would help me. I would meet people who knew exactly where is was coming from and wanted to help me learn to be different and get nothing in return. Opportunities would pop up that I would have never been considered for before.
People would give of themselves freely. I later learned that this is the key to true human value. Giving of myself to others makes me feel amazing. Raising my kids with love and compassion makes me feel proud of being the parent I am. Showing up early to work everyday is an esteem able act and I've been doing it for 15 years so my self-esteem has grown.

We have all helped people and have felt good about it at some point.

7 HOW MUCH WORK IS IT?

I'm not going to lie about this, it takes a lot of work.

I have found the hardest thing I've had to do is wait for the effects of the work I've done to pay off.

Sometime the hardest thing to do is to do nothing.

Early on when I was bored I would create drama. Date a crazy person. Get into a fight. Do something to make me feel that adrenaline. Usually something that would have a consequence tied to it.

Now I ride dirt bikes, ride jet skis, play with my kids, play guitar, play drums, fish, paint. Any number of things that I enjoy.

The work is long and sometimes difficult. Sometimes emotional and I've cried about my upbringing because it wasn't pretty.

But I don't live there anymore. Life is simple now. It's not perfect but after what I've been through it pretty easy.

Do the work and see what happens.

I promise it will be worth it.

If you don't do the work, say hey to the fellas and good luck at 4th draw.

.

Printed in Great Britain
by Amazon

76474985R00031